I0475473

Leadership & the Tao

A new look at the timeless question
"What is Leadership?"

Dr David Tuffley

To my beloved Nation of Four
Concordia Domi – Foris Pax

Management is doing things right;
leadership is doing the right things.
--Peter F. Drucker

Published 2023 by Altiora Publications
AltioraPublications.com/
ISBN: 9781456302412

David Tuffley is a leading authority on the arcane wisdom of the Tao te Ching. At 3,500 years old, it is perhaps the oldest book still in print anywhere in the world. David's modern translation of this ancient work by Lao Tzu in plain English brings its wisdom to a 21st Century readership. David also completed his PhD at Griffith University looking deeply into the nature of leadership. It became apparent that the Tao te Ching is itself a leadership manual.

Acknowledgements

Special thanks are due to my partner Angela for her unwavering support and encouragement. Also to John and Nicola for listening patiently as we drove the long drive between Redland Bay and Brisbane on school days.

Contents

Contents

Contents

Chapter 1 The essence of Leadership

Much has been written since the times of ancient Greece about the nature of leadership. Yet despite the sustained interest in understanding leadership, there are still almost as many definitions of leadership as there are writers on the subject.

Why is this? One explanation is that there is an underlying set of personality traits and competencies that if present in a person will be perceived by those around them as leadership. You cannot see Leadership directly, only the behavior that is informed by those qualities.

The form that these traits take depends on the circumstances in which they are expressed. Since no two set of circumstances are exactly the same, the leadership behavior will also differ, hence the difficulty in agreeing on a single definition.

If leadership qualities cannot be directly perceived, only the behavior that is informed by those qualities, we must look beneath the surface and identify those traits that are embedded deep in human nature, and which have probably not changed for thousands of years.

This book aims to give you an understanding of the underlying principles of leadership by discussing what Lao Tzu has to say, together with perspectives from Social and Evolutionary Psychology. .

Chapter 2 The Tao of Leadership

The essence of leadership is to see a compelling future and then communicating your vision of that future in a way that creates enthusiasm.

The Taoist perspective is useful with this since it cultivates a strong awareness of the patterns of Nature and how these influence human societies. With this awareness you can extrapolate these patterns into the future and see what is possible or likely. But the future is not set in stone. Its direction is influenced by the visionaries and their ability to make their vision a reality.

Consider for example the visions of the future created by the early science fiction writers Jules Verne and H.G. Wells. Generations of engineers have been inspired by the works of Verne and Wells, producing all manner of technologies from submarines called *Nautilus* that could travel 20,000 leagues under the sea without surfacing, journeys to the moon and back, and the exploration of Mars. Later sci-fi writers like Philip K. Dick and William Gibson have also had a profound effect on the direction of technology development. Form and content aside, all of these writers imagined a compelling future and communicated it to the world with impact.

Regardless of whether you are a manager of other people, or someone who has less formal relationships with those around you, the principles discussed in this chapter describe the Taoist way of influencing people. Lao Tzu wrote the Tao

Te Ching specifically for those who might help create a better world, those whose position in society was to lead. By default, the Tao Te Ching is a Leadership manual, albeit one that ranges far and wide into all aspects of life itself.

Introduction to the Tao Te Ching

To help you find the Middle Path, the Tao Te Ching (The Book of the Tao) is an excellent source of insight. The book describes a force called the Tao that operates uniformly throughout the universe and is the causal agent of everything that happens. It explains how you can develop personal power through being in harmony with the Tao.

Written nearly 2,500 years ago, the Tao Te Ching is acknowledged to be a work of the most profound depth, though written in deceptively short, simple chapters numbering only 81 in total. It is one of most translated books in history, with well over 50 translations in English alone. The Tao Te Ching exercises a powerfully transformative effect on those who contemplate it.

The Tao Te Ching is said to have been written by Lao Tzu, the Custodian of the Imperial Archives during the reign of the Chou Dynasty, though some researchers believe that Lao Tzu, which translates as the honorific term *Old Master* is a composite of several people. This practice is not unheard of in the world of literary classics.

Whether Lao Tzu was one man or several, the Tao Te Ching is clearly a reaction to a time of great political unrest. China was comprised of hundreds of warring states that came into frequent conflict with each other in a ceaseless struggle for dominance. Aggression was met with escalating aggression until it seemed the Middle Kingdom would become a wasteland. The Tao Te Ching was written for an audience of leaders and people of influence so they might be guided in the ways of peace and harmony with Nature.

The Tao Te Ching is the result of the author's careful observations of the unfolding patterns of Nature. From these observations a set of underlying principles was deduced that cause the world to behave in the way it does. These principles are in the abstract, in the same way that a mathematical formula is an abstraction. Knowledge of these principles is tremendously helpful for a person seeking harmony and balance, just as the mathematical formula *Pi r squared* is helpful for calculating the area of a circle, any circle.

Lao Tzu came to discern the dynamically interconnected relationship of all things. He then distilled his observations into this modest little book. He called this unifying field of forces the Tao (or the *Way* in English). The Tao Te Ching is therefore something of an ancient Chinese Physics treatise.

The abstraction of the Tao is difficult to express in purely logical terms, so the author resorted to paradox in much the same way as Zen Koans do. This induces an intuitive understanding that complements logical awareness.

An important principle in this unifying field of forces is *polarity*. Lao Tzu's understanding of how the Universe began matches closely what we today would recognise as the Big Bang theory. Before the bang, there was 'The Supreme Absolute' which had limitless undifferentiated potential but no physical existence. Then, in the instant of the bang the Supreme Absolute divided itself from non-existence in an event that created space and time and which is characterised by on-going cause and effect phenomena. This physical universe is founded upon two charged states, yin (negative) and yang (positive). Due to the complementary polarity of matter and energy, these constantly separate and regroup to create the changing, evolving physical reality that is the universe we know.

Everything in the phenomenal universe comes into existence through the dynamically interacting polarities of yin and yang. The way that yin and yang interact is governed by the laws of physics, which Lao Tzu called the Tao. Thus we can view the Tao as an indication of the larger purpose of the Supreme Absolute. Lao Tzu reasoned that if the Absolute wanted to experience itself by creating a universe in which multitudes of conscious points-of-presence create experiences by interacting with each other, then our purpose (as points-of-presence) should be to help the Absolute get a good look at itself by investigating, observing, and emulating Nature.

Taoists therefore work to become aware of and understand the laws of Nature with a view to harmonising with them, particularly as they manifest in human society. The enlightened person cultivates their understanding of the Tao and lives in harmony with Nature.

The six sections and 81 sub-sections that follow are the chapters of the Tao Te Ching organised into six broad categories. These categories were not present in the original Tao Te Ching, and have been added to give a higher-level understanding of the book's content beyond what is normally seen:

- Knowing the Tao

- Using the Tao to become more conscious'

- Using the Tao to cultivate oneself

- Using the Tao to lead

- Using the Tao to influence group dynamics

- Using the Tao to refrain from action

Knowing the Tao

Lao Tzu often describes the behaviour and mindset of the *enlightened person*, by which he means the standard we should aspire to and follow in order to become an effective person in general, including being an effective leader. The enlightened person is wise in the ways of the Tao, and has learned to live in harmony with it.

Below is a faithful rendering into 21st Century language of the original 81 chapters of the Tao Te Ching, which was expressed in a miracle of brevity in just 5,000 Chinese characters.

What is the Tao?

The Tao is analogous to the laws of Physics, which exist only as abstractions. The Tao cannot be seen directly, but its effects can be observed in the world of forms, hence the saying from the Tao Te Ching *the Tao that can be seen is not the real Tao*. The mathematical formula for calculating the area of a circle is pi (22 divided by 7) multiplied by the square of the radius of the circle. This formula is an abstraction that can be applied to any circle at any scale of magnitude from an atom up to the universe itself. The formula is an example of the Tao expressed in the language of Physics.

Another example from Physics is Isaac Newton's second law of motion; *the mutual forces of action and reaction between two bodies are equal, opposite and collinear*. In the Tao Te Ching, this principle is discussed many times. Essentially, the enlightened person understands the operation of this law in the social sphere and ensures that any action they take is done with full awareness of the likely reactions, or, they refrain from taking action altogether.

In a general sense, the Tao can be understood as the agent by which forms evolve. It is a pervasive, underlying influence that evolves one form into its own opposite and then back again in an on-going cycle of alternating polar opposites.

Alignment with the subtle

An enlightened person works constantly to establish the Tao in their awareness, and to harmonise their mind and body with the Tao. They do not use force to achieve their ends because they know that to do so is likely to cause an equal and opposite reaction. In this way they avoid a problem of their own making.

Instead, they work at the level of underlying cause and with little apparent effort are able to bring about the outcome they want. The enlightened person therefore knows that when they are in step with the Tao in worldly affairs, their endeavours can be completed without adverse effects.

Using what is not there

Just as doors and windows cut into a wall are what make a room useful, the enlightened person knows how to use what is not there in a given situation to create a desirable effect. They create a sense of absence in a situation that the forces of Nature are compelled to resolve, in the same way that air rushes in to fill a vacuum.

The essence

The essence of the Tao is formless, nameless and intangible, therefore it can only be perceived by the intuitive mind, not by the analytical mind. The enlightened person works to integrate both intuitive and analytical aspects of their whole mind to arrive at a comprehensive understanding of the Tao. With an intuitive understanding of the patterns of life, they can subtly influence the outcome of events.

You do not have a life, you *are* life

The millions of life-forms on this planet -- animal and plant -- are all instances of the same life-force. This life- force lives *through* each life-form. We are possessed by the life-force, rather being the possessor of the life-force, which is an expression of the Tao. All life-forms are subject equally to the laws of Nature that govern life -- all are born, gather strength, reach a peak, go into decline and then die. No exceptions, only variations in outer form and the duration of the lifecycle. The same can be said of the weather, politics, relationships and everything else in the observable world.

These laws of Nature -- the Tao -- are also expressed on a higher level in our minds and in the patterns of our social behaviour. Enlightened people gain influence by learning to recognise and live in harmony with these underlying laws of Nature. That way, they can predict future trends and take early action, placing them in the right place at the right time.

The origins of creativity

The Tao that underlies and gives shape to space and time in the world of form is the same state that preceded the Big Bang. As such it is a potent creative force. The enlightened person cultivates their creativity by identifying with the Absolute - the creative state that exists outside of time and space and which preceded the Big Bang. This can be done by regular meditation practice.

Greatness

The Tao is great because it is cyclic. It causes everything in Nature to behave cyclically. Given enough time, patterns of events repeat themselves, hence the expression 'history repeats'. The power of Taoism lies in perceiving and understanding the patterns of change and aligning oneself with them. Enlightened people intuitively perceive the evolution of society. With sufficient patience they are able to guide themselves and others towards harmony and fulfilment. This idea is expressed by T.S. Eliot in his poem

Little Gidding; *we shall never cease from exploration, and the end of all our exploring, will be to arrive where we started, and know the place for the first time.*

An evolutionary force

The Tao is an informing principle that permeates everything in the physical world, giving it structure and prescribing behavioural patterns. Over time, this informing principle interacts dynamically with the environment resulting in evolutionary changes in those life-forms as they become better adapted to their environment.

Enlightened people who express the Tao and allow it to work through them are perceived to have charisma. Others naturally respond to this charisma with a willingness to be influenced by the enlightened person. Lao Tzu believed that to emulate the behaviour of the Tao in one's own behaviour would bring a person into the closest possible alignment with reality. A life that shares, in its aims, the purpose of the universe, will also share in its greatness and significance. The enlightened person's life comes to embody the universe and charismatically demonstrates that the macrocosm (universe) is reflected in the microcosm (person).

Polarity

The Tao operates through polarity, the physical law that governs cause and effect. The law of polarity is similar to Newton's third law of motion in which every action has an equal and opposite reaction that is prescribed by the initiating cause. An initiating event in time morphs into its own opposite. A pendulum swings to one side, then to the other. In human terms this manifests in such cycles as war and peace, economic boom and bust, ignorance and enlightenment. The law of polarity changes and evolves all things by reducing extremes back to a more moderate state on its way to the opposite extreme. Extremes are by definition overcharged and must begin moving in the opposite direction. Those who follow the Tao therefore work hard to avoid extremes. They practice moderation and openness to change as a way of life.

Proactive not reactive

The enlightened person looks for the seeds of change, the underlying triggers of change that will tell them what is likely to happen in the future. Guiding them is their awareness that everything in the phenomenal world will be transformed into its own opposite in time. For example birth to death, happy to sad, strong to weak, day to night. In this way, they come to understand the movement of polarity in its countless manifestations, and so gain penetrating insight into worldly affairs. The enlightened person can proactively use this insight to position themselves favourably for when the future arrives.

For example, when we look at European history from the year 1000 to 2000, we see a pattern of aggregation. From a multitude of small states in the 11th Century has emerged a unified Europe in the 21st Century. Through cycles of war and peace, ignorance and enlightenment, plague and prosperity we see the numerous smaller states becoming increasingly aggregated, for example the unification of the

German States under Bismarck and again in 1990 after the collapse of the Soviet Union. This movement of the Tao from war to peace to war many times has evolved Europe into a unified entity, at least at an economic level. In the 21st Century this unification process is extending East to Russia and the Islamic world and South to the shores of Africa, areas not previously thought of as 'European'. Given this trend towards unification, an enlightened person might reasonably predict that the European Union will continue to incorporate non-EU states until it becomes necessary to change the name 'European' or at least redefine what 'Europe' means.

Another example is the rise and fall of political and commercial empires. History has many examples of empires that began modestly, grew powerful, and then declined when their power became over-extended.

Using the Tao is about understanding the patterns of the past, extrapolating them into the future and using this information to guide our actions in the present. In this way, we can to some extent influence the course of future events.

The ineffable cause

Every culture has some concept of the Ineffable (that which defies logical definition) whose purpose is to describe the underlying cause of the universe and the world as we know it. The Tao *is* that ineffable cause regardless of the name it is given.

The metaphor of a flowing river in which we all swim is often used to describe the Tao, whose movement can be seen at many levels. There is the flow of life from one day to the next, the flow of human history measured in centuries, and the flow of evolution itself, measured in millions of years. The enlightened person seeks detachment by concentrating on the Tao, the underlying cause of the flow, and not on the phenomena that are caused by the Tao.

The patterns of Nature

Enlightened people ceaselessly observe the patterns of Nature and work to bring their own behaviour into alignment with those patterns. Over time, the enlightened person's knowledge of these patterns evolves into an integrated model. This model informs their world-view with a vast network of connections that brings them into close alignment with the ways of Nature, which by definition leads to a condition of least resistance to the world.

Using the Tao to become more conscious

This section explores the action of the Tao as it manifests in human awareness. By working to bring one's awareness of the Tao to a higher level, one's intuitive understanding of the world and the way it works is improved.

The Buddhist concept of Mindfulness is analogous to becoming more aware of the Tao. In cognitive science terms, it is engaging the most recently evolved parts of the human brain to exercise heightened awareness.

Sameness of bearing

The Tao is impartial. It does not play favourites. The human equivalent is *sameness of bearing* in which the enlightened person acts equally, with compassion, towards all people, regardless of rank or status. Sameness of bearing allows the enlightened person to achieve a degree of emotional and intellectual independence from the world, lest they be swayed to favour one person over another, one group over another. An impartial mind-set allows the enlightened person to be in tune with their Intuition -- the inner voice of the Tao and the source of all creativity and enlightenment.

Being non-competitive

The behaviour of enlightened people is often compared to that of water. It is in the nature of water to seek the low places and bring benefits there. Water does not seek the high places; neither does the enlightened person seek high status for its own sake.

The conventional view of success in Western society is a competitive struggle for pre-eminence in a chosen field. A person fights their way as high as they can on the 'slippery pole', climbing over the backs of others in the process. Such competitive behaviour is a form of war-fare in which others are seen as enemies and a person's awareness of the Tao is diminished or absent altogether. They cannot hear their Intuition.

The enlightened person therefore cultivates a non-competitive mindset in which they look for win-win opportunities in their dealings with others. Such a mind-set expands their awareness to the point where they see no need to follow societal conventions in their quest for fulfilment.

Limiting sensual desire

The enlightened person cultivates Intuition by disciplining themselves to limit their desire for sensory experiences. That desire causes suffering is well known as the second noble truth of Buddhism. Freeing oneself of the desire for unnecessary food, drugs, possessions and experiences brings the enlightened person into closer contact with their inner nature.

The enlightened person also limits their desire for the praise and acceptance of others. In so doing, they lessen in direct proportion the fear they might experience at receving the disapproval or blame of others. Praise and blame are two sides of the same coin with which our compliance with group norms is purchased.

Limiting sensual desire and expanding one's awareness to embrace the world brings one's (inner) microcosm into alignment with the (outer) macrocosm. Instead of being consumed by narrow self-interest, the enlightened person's sense of identity expands to encompass the world.

A true win-win situation

The enlightened person raises their consciousness by cultivating a strong desire to *know* the Tao at a deep level. The Tao reciprocates these efforts by meeting the seeker half-way. In the process, both are expanded and merge into one, producing a true win-win situation.

Perhaps this is the origin of the Biblical adage that the *Good Lord helps those that helps themselves.* Philosopher Friedrich Nietzsche put it another way; *If you stare into the Abyss long enough, the Abyss stares back at you.* Abyss in this context implies immense depth, not that there is something sinister lurking there.

Merge with the cycles of Nature

Everything in the universe behaves cyclically. All living creatures and inanimate things have their cycles of existence, and collectively these cycles form a vast, harmonious whole. It is a true miracle to behold. The enlightened person strives to know themselves as blended with this harmonious whole. They try to transcend ordinary egoic consciousness which has them separate from the world, a lone entity in a hostile wilderness.

Instincts and Intuition

In the Taoist view, human instincts are fundamentally good, acting as a link to a person's Intuition. When a person loses contact with their instincts, standards of right-behaviour and morality are created by society to compensate for the resulting social disarray. People are separated from their Intuition when they identify themselves too much with righteous behaviour, morality and patriotism.

Consider the practice of philanthropy. Some of what passes for philanthropy in the world is primarily an attempt to buy people's good opinion of the giver, who is usually a tycoon who has made enemies on their way to financial success. How many high-profile philanthropists would give as much if they were obliged to do so anonymously? True philanthropy does not draw attention to itself.

Contemplating the subtle

Contemplating the Tao does not appeal to the senses. Doing so will seem boring and pointless to the person who lives for sensual gratification and expects to be entertained every minute of the day and night. Yet the enlightened person perseveres with this endeavour, since to do so leads to a mind-expanding glimpse and then a growing vision of the universe as a cohesive, interconnected whole.

For example, contemplating the subtle suggests that since the laws of Physics (or the Tao) have allowed life to evolve on this planet, it is reasonable to conclude that there is life on other planets, since the laws of Physics operate uniformly in the universe. If those laws have caused life to evolve here, then why not elsewhere? As one Astro-Physicist suggests, about one out of every 14,000 planets in our galaxy have conditions similar to those on planet Earth. With billions of planets in the Milky Way, there are millions of planets in this galaxy alone that could support life similar to that on Earth.

Influence without motive

The best kind of influence to exercise in worldly affairs is power without ulterior motive. Such power acts for the greater good, not personal gain. Exercising power for personal gain is perilous, since it often degenerates into the application of force, requiring elaborate strategies and manipulations to succeed and causing repercussions regardless of outcome.

Lao Tzu thought that morality and proprietary behaviour comes about when people are unable to see the truth in themselves, and are therefore incapable of trusting others to find truth in themselves. The problem with these forms of behaviour is that they become an entrenched block to people's ability to access the deeper truths in themselves. Then the behaviour becomes an end in itself, not a means to an end.

The enlightened person does not seek coercive power over others. Such power is ultimately an illusion. They seek instead to become the master of subtle influence which does not appear to be power at all. This influence derives from being in close identification with the deeper reality of the world.

Avoiding extremes and full maturity

When anything reaches its peak, or fullest expression, it is bound to go into decline not long afterwards. The enlightened person avoids pushing anything to an extreme state unless they deliberately want to induce a state of decline. When a vessel is half-full it has further use and potential. When completely full it waits only to be emptied. In general terms, an open-ended situation has the capacity for continued growth.

By avoiding extremes, the enlightened person becomes increasingly centred and tranquil. In this state they are able to contribute positively to the collective awareness of the world, thus expanding their own consciousness in the process.

The flame that burns twice as bright burns half as long

The enlightened person extends their life-span through practicing moderation in all things. They limit what comes in through their senses by avoiding excessive sense stimulation. They know that their life force grows stronger if they use the moderated energy received through their senses for internal growth, so they do not talk or otherwise express too much. They practice moderation so that output does not exceed input, knowing that as life goes out, death comes in.

By nurturing their life force, the enlightened person makes themselves less vulnerable to the dangers of the world. They are protected from harm not through luck but through avoiding the cultivation of weakness. They know that the flame that burns twice as bright burns half as long.

Dwelling at the centre

Through careful observation of the patterns of Nature, the enlightened person comes to perceive the fullness of the Tao. When the Tao is perceived, a person's fears disappear as the mind expands to embrace the interconnected whole.

Lao Tzu suggests that the enlightened person should remain open to the information that comes through their senses from the outside world. They should then use their Intuition to process this moderated input to develop an understanding of the patterns of life. They continually augment their experience of the world with information from their intuitive mind. They live with full awareness of the world, but habitually use Intuition as their main way of understanding the world. They do not rely on theories and ideologies originating from outside to understand the world.

For example, imagine a married man goes into a bar for a drink at the end of the working day. It happens to be a topless bar, and the sight of the barmaid's breasts causes the man want to have sex with her. This information from his senses and his reaction to it could be intuitively understood as Nature giving the man a reason and a desire to reproduce. If the man understands the evolutionary truth of this, he has no reason to feel guilty unless he acts on the desire and breaks his marriage vows. But if he references an external ideology that says such feelings are always guilt-worthy, then his guilt will be added to the by-now crippling store of guilt that he has built up over time. The intuitive man has a clean conscience. The ideologue is burdened with guilt from having had a natural feeling. Who would you rather be? Is it not better to understand life using Intuition rather than an ideology as your primary means of understanding?

Envisaging a better world

The enlightened person expands their awareness by imagining an ideally functioning world with fully conscious people living in well-founded communities. Over time, with effort, this microcosmic view of the world created in the enlightened mind can be transferred and generalised into the macrocosm.

Lao Tzu himself envisaged a world of fully conscious people who are firmly in control of their own destinies and that of the world around them. In this ideal world, all are united into a collective, compassionate entity. The Tao Te Ching is the means by which Lao Tzu is bringing about such a world.

Oneness with the evolving universe

Those who know, don't say; those who say, don't know is an oft-quoted passage from the Tao Te Ching. The enlightened person's understanding of the world comes from their intuitive mind and the natural structures and patterns of the universe as they are microcosmically represented in the person. This understanding is not easily translated into words, so most of the time, the enlightened person is content to simply know it and does not speak of it.

But if a person's understanding of the world is based on ideologies or socio-cultural artefacts of some kind, these have been formalised into words that are spoken often from one to another. This is not to imply that such an understanding is necessarily wrong. It suggests only that such an understanding runs the risk of being out of date, or incomplete, or misunderstood.

The enlightened person therefore expands their awareness by cultivating an intellectual independence that resists external influences. They realise their oneness with the evolving universe through unwavering simplicity and inner truth.

The disease

There is a common stereotype in today's world of the highly educated specialist who has little interest in other people's opinions because they believe they know everything already. The enlightened person knows that regardless of how knowledgeable they are, there is much they do not know, and will probably never know, so vast is the total amount of knowledge accumulated by humanity over time. So they maintain a certain humility about their erudition and remain open to new information from the changing world regardless of the relative status of the person imparting that information.

In the Taoist view, it is considered most unfortunate to be unaware of one's ignorance, whether in interpersonal matters, worldly affairs or within the self. So the enlightened person cultivates the attitude of the beginner who knows little and is open to new ideas from a constantly evolving universe that they are yet to experience.

By maintaining this beginner's attitude, the enlightened person avoids the inevitable decline that comes from being too full to grow any further.

Using the Tao to cultivate oneself

The enlightened person lowers their expectations to the point where they are rarely if ever disappointed. They free themselves of their pre-conceived ideas and any ideologies that might limit their growth.

In Buddhism, attachment to impermanent forms is recognised as the source of all suffering. Expectations can be seen as a form of attachment to a certain outcome.

The pendulum of polarity

The enlightened person understands that the world of form is characterised by polar opposites that oscillate back and forth between the two ends of the same continuum. It is not possible to have one without the other. When beauty is present, ugliness is not far away. Youth gives way to maturity. Happiness turns into sadness. Wealth to poverty. Arrogance to humility. The Sufi proverb *This too shall pass* expresses this essential truth with simplicity.

The enlightened person also knows that matter becomes energy and vice versa. All of the physical forms in the world, in the universe, will cease to exist in a physical sense one day and return to energy only to revert to matter again at a later time.

Descending from the peak

When the enlightened person achieves success, they do not *rest on their laurels* and wait for the inevitable decline. Instead they move quickly on to the next challenge and continue their growth even though this involves descending from the peak that was so laboriously attained, down into the valley that lies before the next peak. They avoid accumulating social ties and/or material possessions, all of which can reduce their ability to move on to the next challenge.

Moderating the dynamic tension between polar opposites

Human nature is comprised of a complex set of oscillating polar opposites. These can push and pull a person about, contributing to the drama and sometimes chaos in their lives.

The enlightened person works hard to moderate the extremes of these oscillations, endeavouring to stabilise them on or near the Middle Path, thus creating a calm inner space in which contemplation can occur. This is an essential skill for the enlightened person.

Subtle influence

The enlightened person develops their ability to perceive and understand an unfolding situation at a deep level. They take no action unless they have first come to this understanding. The only way they can do this is to harmonise their inner self with the outer situation, aligning their inner reality with the outer.

Having perceived the unfolding pattern, the enlightened person moves forwards with a modesty and a stability that causes no counter reactions. The less obvious their actions are, the more effective they become. To the world they appear to be reserved. They channel their influence to bring clarity and cooperation into the world.

For example, if a dictator seizes power in a *coup d'etat*, the natural tendency is for the people resist and the dictator must spent considerable energy dealing with this reaction to his initial action. If, on the other hand, he were to work quietly, from within the existing government to bring about evolutionary change, it would barely be recognised by the people and the change of government would seem like a natural progression.

Independent perspective

Lao Tzu suggests that having an independent perspective is vital for spiritual growth. The enlightened person keeps their own counsel, removing themselves from situations where group-think exerts its influence.

With independence of thought they shed their misgivings and can explore the universe with no preconceived ideas. Independence of thought means divesting oneself of ideological thinking and orthodox sets of belief. It takes courage to do this. Humans tend to be social creatures with a powerful instinct for group-thinking, a vestige of our evolutionary past where there was safety in numbers. The person who moves out of the orthodoxy is likely to be punished by the group for their non-conformist thinking. Often this will be enough to bring the person back into the fold where it is comfortable and secure. But at some level they know they have traded their freedom for this security.

Unhindered by group-think and with a clear perception of the world as it is, the enlightened person makes a significant contribution to the collective awareness of human-kind. They see the likely future by extrapolating upon the patterns of the past. As Einstein observed *We can not solve problems by using the same kind of thinking we used when we created them.*

Observing the patterns of Nature

Lao Tzu noticed that the patterns of Nature are evident in socio-cultural behaviour. For example the pattern of cause and effect is clearly evident everywhere in Nature *and* in the social environment. The enlightened person works hard to transcend cause and effect by practicing moderation. For example, an obvious attempt to gain power is avoided, since to do so is likely to produce a neutralising effect in the social environment. The enlightened person exerts influence by channelling the inner power that comes from having a universal awareness. They achieve their objectives by avoiding showy outer appearances.

Through this practice, enlightened people develop what might be called intellectual gravity, the exercise of which can determine the direction of society. The stronger the gravity, the greater the influence will be.

The conventional wisdom of society encourages people to display themselves. Yet such a display is by definition excessive. In Nature excess is naturally reduced. The enlightened person realises it is ill-advised to seek prominence. It is better to exert subtle influence behind the scenes. In this way, they achieve stability and longevity. By working behind the scenes, the laws of Nature do not act to reduce their position.

For example, consider the musician Kurt Cobain. He became famous, but found the fame intolerable. He had become that which he despised. To Kurt, the only way to resolve his dilemma was to commit suicide. Celebrity status did not bring happiness or enlightenment, just intolerable sadness that could only be resolved through oblivion.

Steady, incremental improvement

Steady, incremental improvement, as a general rule, is preferable to sudden intense effort. The former can be sustained for long periods, the latter quickly leads to exhaustion. The enlightened person therefore acts sustainably and avoids confrontation or aggressive movement towards their objectives. They know that in Nature, the sudden intense storm is the exception to the rule, that most of the time Nature operates in a steady, harmonious way that brings about gradual transformation, almost imperceptibly. They practice steady, incremental improvement over time, and achieve their objectives harmoniously.

Cultivating the steady force of positive attitude and expressing it modestly gives the enlightened person a degree of personal power. They know that what they think and believe is what they will become, in time.

Mastery of self

Insight into the underlying causal patterns beneath socio-cultural phenomena can be had through self-knowledge and self-discipline. The enlightened person works hard to know their inner mind. In time, they come to see the connection with the evolving mind of the universe. With self-mastery, the enlightened person can make a lasting contribution to society.

Self-mastery and the insight that follows gives the enlightened person the ability to change the world through small, effortless actions at the beginning of events before the situation has become more settled. A prime example is a wise and benevolent parent giving their impressionable child much information about the world and how it works at a time when the child is still open to such messages. This effort by the parent for 10 or more years sets the child up for the rest of their life, perhaps another 70 years.

Needing less

Material possessions *can* be an impediment to spiritual growth. The problem is not in the having of possessions *per se*. The problem arises when a person *identifies* with their possessions, creating a sense of identity like a King identifying with his palaces and kingdom. Their intellectual growth is slowed because the forms which occupy their thinking are relatively unchanging. They are required to spend considerable effort in maintaining those forms, and preventing the theft of them. Over time, materialistic people come to regard the world as being fixed into specific forms, rather than fluid and evolving as in Nature. The enlightened person therefore does not create an identity for themselves from their possessions. They know that by doing so, they reduce their ability to move freely with the spirit of the times.

Animals and plants display the power in needing less. They have little except their lives and the environment that sustains them. They are in harmony with the Tao and need nothing more for their survival.

Keeping an open mind

A mind that remains open to new information on a moment by moment basis is a pre-requisite for spiritual growth. A person seeking enlightenment works daily to overcome the all-too-human tendency to settle into an established belief system that they have been investing in for years or decades. The more invested a person feels themselves to be, the more closed-minded they become to information that does not agree with their beliefs, or threatens those beliefs in some way.

Such a belief system may have been correct in the past, but in an evolving social environment those ideas probably need of updating. An open mind stays in harmony with the collective mind of society and the universe. It is from this position of openness and harmony with the universe that the enlightened person acts upon the world in a way that does not create negative reactions.

Lao Tzu speaks of a powerful transformative practice. By loving people who do not love themselves, the enlightened person emulates the Tao and neutralises the negative attitudes of others. Lao Tzu considered that the ability to neutralise extremes in their various forms is the way to transform the world into a more peaceful place.

The mind of humanity, the group mind, is an intermediate step between our individual minds and the universal mind. The group mind is a stepping stone that the enlightened person can use to perceive the larger universal mind. It allows them to go beyond and see themselves in relation to the universe. They merge their individual mind with the group mind by first *opening* their mind, and allowing their sense of identity, their ego, to be diminished. The difficulty is that the ego protects itself with a host of effective defence mechanisms.

Dwelling in the Tao

Since only the ruling elite could read, the Tao Te Ching was written for an exclusive readership; people whose destiny was to lead or otherwise influence worldly affairs. The book teaches how to cultivate Intuition. With an intuitive understanding, the reader could perceive the evolution of society and be in a position to positively influence that evolution. It should be remembered that China at the time of writing was a war-torn land.

Remaining flexible and adaptable

The enlightened person recognises from his or her observations of Nature that flexibility and adaptability is necessary for long-term survival. The universe is evolving, and everything in it is changing. Therefore people who hold fixed, orthodox beliefs are not likely to react appropriately to new challenges.

Imagine a sapling tree growing on a wind-swept hill. Nearby is the sapling's mature parent. When the winter gales blow, the young tree bends. After the storm, it resumes its upright position. But the old tree has become inflexible, unable to bend. One day, it simply breaks and falls over, never to rise again.

On a human level, young people display adaptability to their world that allows them to respond resiliently to the events that come their way. But as they grow older, some of them become overly attached to their youth and resist the change happening around them. They are heard complaining about the state of the world, and how they would like to go back to the 'good old days'. These are the same good old days when parents and teachers physically assaulted their children 'for their own good', when husbands beat their wives as a matter of course.

As they age, they resemble the inflexible old tree and its inevitable collapse in the face of some adversity. But it need not be the case. An enlightened elderly person accepts the need to change with the times. They are prepared to let go of out-moded beliefs, and are willing to expend the effort to learn new skills. They do not criticise the younger generation simply for being young and believing differently than they do. In short, they make the effort to stay young when it is easier to allow oneself to grow old.

The great leveller of extremes

The enlightened person has observed Nature's way of levelling extremes. An example on a grand scale is the magnificent Himalayan Mountains. Through tectonic movement of the Earth's crust the Himalayas were raised. The mountains reach great heights above the plain, but through the movement of the Tao over millions of years, the mountains are being worn away by the weather. Melting snow erodes the mountainsides each year. Billions of tonnes of alluvium then wash down the Ganges and Brahmaputra rivers, settling in the spreading delta and out into the Bay of Bengal. What was high is now low.

An animal that breeds too prolifically and becomes a plague is naturally reduced to smaller numbers in time. In human affairs, a tyrant eventually gets their come-uppance. Everywhere in Nature is found this moderating effect of the Tao. At the molecular level, atoms form bonds with each other that allow for the mutual reduction of excess electrical charge.

The enlightened person uses this principle to safe-guard their own position while they go about their work of improving society. In order for energy to flow in their direction, they maintain a modestly reduced position by being humble in their dealings with others and avoiding shows of ostentation.

For example, if someone with sufficient means were to quietly donate $1,000 a month to an international welfare agency, they might bring on-going benefit to perhaps 1,000 people in the developing world in the form of clean drinking water, agriculture, schools, basic hospital care etc. This anonymous gift would be greatly appreciated by the mother who has already lost a baby to dysentery. The same $1,000 might also be used to buy a flashy consumer item, luxury car perhaps, for the purpose of raising their status in the eyes of their peers. The enlightened person sees the relative merit in these two scenarios.

Being magnanimous

When the enlightened person has power over others, they know to act with generosity and compassion. Not gloating over their advantage avoids the possibility of lingering resentment that may adversely affect their future dealings.

35

Through generosity, they create a mind-set of appreciation and agreement in people, the better for collaborative endeavours.

Living for the maximum benefit of others

Simple, plain truth that is not embellished with sophistry and rhetoric is unlikely to become distorted. The enlightened person therefore maintains an attitude of simplicity. They conduct their affairs and express themselves with simplicity. This attitude cultivates a mind-set that sees clearly the truth in a given situation. They allow their actions to speak for themselves, knowing that people instinctively know that a person's actions speak louder than their words.

Simplicity extends to not hoarding static accumulations of possessions or money for the love of having them, rather than using them for worthwhile purposes. The enlightened person avoids hoarding and keeps the flow of energy moving through their life. By not accumulating an extreme amount, they do not invite the levelling effect of the Tao.

The enlightened person lives to do the maximum good in the most unobtrusive way. Their reward is not honours and recognition from society but the deep satisfaction of knowing that one is emulating the Tao and is thereby in harmony with it.

Using the Tao to lead

A central idea in Taoism is avoiding extremes and always seeking the middle path on our journey through life. The objective is to negotiate the middle ground between opposites or extremes so effectively that no act is followed by a reaction. The net effect is one of neutrality. Finding the middle path means not needing to suffer the consequences of an act. In terms of the doctrine of Karma, it means knowing how to avoid bad reactions, or bad karma.

Effective leadership requires you to live in this way so that you do not swing like a pendulum from one drama to the next, creating disturbances in your life that get in the way of calm inner reflection. It is finding the Middle Path. The Tao Te Ching encourages us to sense the world around you directly and to contemplate your impressions deeply. It advises against relying on the structures and belief systems that have been created by others and put forward as orthodox truth. Such ideologies remove you from a direct experience of life and effectively cut you off from your Intuition. Lao Tzu believed that Intuition is the only way that you can truly *know* the world; from an experiential rather than intellectual position.

The Middle Path requires you to develop an awareness of the physical forces that shape your world and direct its events. Such forces operate uniformly at all levels, from the macrocosm to the microcosm. They operate in the universe as a whole and in the minds and lives of individual people. An understanding of these natural laws and the forces they direct gives you the power to direct events in the world without resorting to force, by using attitude instead of action.

Influence on others is achieved through guiding rather than ruling. The objective is always to avoid taking action that will elicit counter-reactions. In Nature, an excessive force in a particular direction tends to trigger the growth of an opposing force, and therefore the use of force cannot be the basis for establishing an enduring social condition.

The enlightened leader comes to understand that everything in the universe is in a state of flux, and that the emotional and intellectual structures that we like to build for ourselves in order to feel secure and to understand the world are likewise subject to change by external forces that are largely beyond our control. The challenge is to accept the inevitability of change and not waste our energy trying to prop up these impermanent structures, defending them against criticisms, and trying to convince others to believe in them so that they might become recognised as permanent truth.

Grasping the reality of the impermanence of all structures allows you to align yourself with the forces of Nature that bring about incremental change in the social and physical world. You can embrace and support change whenever and wherever it wants to occur. Your alignment with the forces in Nature makes you a part of those forces. Your perceptual processes become more finely tuned because they are based on evolving reality, not on orthodox thinking. You see the world as it is, not as you believe it should be.

Finding the Middle Path and keeping to it is how the enlightened leader must arrange their life so that enough peace and tranquillity exists in their inner world for their Intuition to develop and become a guiding influence. A person whose life is chaotic, lurching from one disaster to the next in a constant state of crisis is not in a state of mind conducive to effective leadership.

The steady force of attitude

Leading by example is the most desirable form of leadership. The enlightened leader understands that it is the steady force of their attitudes, as perceived by those around them, that exerts the greatest influence, more so than their actions or their words. Through example, people come to know what a leader respects and values. These values become the motivating force behind people's actions. The enlightened leader therefore models high regard for honesty, flexibility and spontaneity.

The enlightened leader avoids championing high-achievers. They know that by creating one winner, they simultaneously create multiple losers who then feel under-valued. High achievers should be *quietly* congratulated and rewarded. Singling high-achievers out for public praise creates what Stephen Covey calls a scarcity mentality. The praise of the leader is a scarce commodity that is reserved for the favoured few.

The enlightened leader brings peace and stability to the group through the steady force of their positive attitudes. They do not micro-manage, allowing people to get on with their activities without interference.

Subtle influence

According to Lao Tzu, the best kind of leader is one whose existence is barely known by those they lead. The next best are loved, the next are respected and the next are ridiculed.

The enlightened leader avoids coercion, instead they use subtle influence (like goal-setting, trust and carefully worded directives) so that the people are barely aware of their influence. The worst thing a leader can do is adopt and overbearing approach in which people perceive that they are being interfered with at some level and their need for autonomy over how they perform their work is disregarded. This is sure to generate negative reaction.

Subtle influence allows a person to develop autonomy from which they derive the satisfaction of one who manages their own affairs.

Maintaining simplicity

Simple, intuitively-derived ways of behaving that are in tune with the Tao are preferable to socially-defined behaviour protocols. It is all too easy with the latter to make mistakes and give unintentional offence. Correct behaviour protocols create in-groups and out-groups, those who know how to behave correctly, and the uncouth oafs who do not. It plays into the egoic tendency to categorise the world as *us and them, friend and enemy*. Simple, intuitively based leadership is likely to be more inclusive and compassionate, seeking commonality between people rather than points of difference.

Modes of social behaviour that are considered praiseworthy, such as self-seeking philanthropy, should be avoided. Self-seeking behaviour of any kind is primarily done for social recognition that then feeds back to improved self-esteem. It is an indication that Intuition is not being used and the person needs an external source to tell them what is right and good. The enlightened leader, in tune with their Intuition, practices anonymous philanthropy and enhances their self-esteem directly.

The enlightened leader therefore acts with humility and remains in close contact with their instincts. They keep their thoughts and actions simple and spontaneous. With this mind-set, they are more agile and appropriate in their responses to emerging situations. Simplicity endows power through clarity of meaning. People intuitively perceive the enlightened leader's alignment with the Tao.

The enlightened leader therefore throws off the constraints of orthodoxy and tradition, using these only in a secondary sense, if at all. Orthodoxy can be a straight-jacket for the imagination. It constrains creativity and limits spontaneity. A tradition-bound leader will tend to base their decisions on precedent *what did my predecessors do in this situation* or *in 1793, our illustrious leader did this in response to a similar situation?*. These prefabricated responses lack insight and run a high risk of not being appropriate for the situation at hand.

Gravitas

Gravitas or force of personality can exercise strong influence on people, so it is wise to know how to cultivate it. Gravitas is manifested in the enlightened leader as they become more closely aligned with the Tao. Such alignment naturally deepens and endows perceived substance to their personality.

It has been observed that the worth of a nation, or organisation or individual can be known by how they treat the weakest member of their group. Observe how a person treats those over whom they have power. Do they treat them with consideration and respect, or are they harsh because they can be? The enlightened leader knows that treating everyone with simple dignity endows their actions with subtle but powerful influence; the underlying quality of gravitas. Author John Steinbeck demonstrated true leadership with his Nobel Prize winning novel *The Grapes of Wrath* (1939). In contrast, French Queen Marie-Antoinette from her privileged position showed contemptuous disregard for the welfare of the people with her *let them eat cake* comment. Though probably a journalistic cliché it sums up the attitude of the French aristocracy that so enraged the people and led to the French Revolution in 1789.

Enlightened leaders do not use their position to grant themselves special rewards not available to everyone, for example executive bonuses that are many times the annual salary of ordinary employees. The simple dignity of the servant leader is most conducive to achieving their objectives.

Coordinating collective effort

Enlightened leadership is seen where the talents and abilities of a diverse set of people can be coordinated into a unified effort. Such leadership is about creating an environment in which people can network and exchange ideas in pursuit of common objectives. The leader is like a lake that collects and contains water. They modestly provide the environment in which people can work together and exchange ideas in pursuit of common objectives. Their influence is so pervasive and subtle that people stop noticing it.

Intuitive leaders therefore have the ability to unite people with diverse backgrounds into a single enterprise, thus creating a direct link between people whose only previous connection was so tenuous as to be almost invisible. The enlightened leader perceives these subtle connections and builds networks out of them. In this way, they behave like the Tao.

Guide rather than rule

It is well-known that people dislike being forced to do anything. They prefer freedom to choose, or at least the appearance of freedom. So even when an enlightened leader has the authority to order people about, they avoid doing so. They know it is better to guide people to a course of action by giving them a reason to want to do it. As Dwight Eisenhower remarked, leadership *is the art of getting people to do what you want them to do because they want to do it*. The enlightened leader does this by presenting the case in such a way that the course of action is clearly in the person's best interest and/or the greater interests of the group they serve.

Cultivating one-ness

The enlightened leader recognises the inter-connectedness of all things in the universe and cultivates a sense of solidarity and oneness with people. This oneness is a state of felt awareness and harmony between the one and the many. The enlightened leader works daily to cultivate and maintain this sense of felt connectedness with everything. It gives insight into the rhythms and patterns of the Universe and informs the enlightened leader's every action.

Unity of effort

Unity of effort is achieved when the enlightened leader creates enthusiasm for their vision of the future. They put the right person in the job, provide the resources they need, the authority to make decisions, then stand back and let them do the work without unnecessary restrictions.

Lao Tzu believed that people are basically good at heart, only becoming aggressive and unruly in reaction to unreasonable force or perceived injustice. The enlightened leader therefore fosters a collaborative environment based on fairness and behaves with simplicity and modesty. They avoid creating unnecessary internal competition which works against collaboration by encouraging people to pursue strategies to gain advantage at the expense of others.

Replace rigid rules with spontaneity

Some organisations operate with rigidly defined rules that everyone must conform to if they are not to be punished. This approach offends human nature that is angered by unreasonable force. The consequence is that the people grow resentful and look for ways to subvert the orthodoxy, and they will usually succeed at this. When management perceives the trend, they react by exerting more pressure. The people react even more strongly, and a negative cycle of behaviour is created.

Rigidly defined rules are a form of extremism that produces sharply polarised attitudes. These attitudes are likely to be counter-productive by reducing the desire to collaborate freely. The enlightened leader knows how polarity operates in Nature, and so the avoid such extremes. They achieve their objectives without confrontation, projecting a straight-forward, down-to-earth honesty that inspires trust and confidence in people, and which provides a model for the people to emulate.

Like cooking a small fish

Leading a large organisation is like cooking a small fish. This enigmatic statement conveys the need for an enlightened leader to maintain a light, delicate touch in their leadership in the same way as it is necessary to avoid too much stirring when cooking a small fish, lest the fish fall apart in the pan. When an organisation is experiencing challenges, too much action from the leader will unbalance the situation, making it worse.

The enlightened leader knows that if there is no simple solution to a problem, it is best to simply let it be and allow the forces of Nature to evolve a solution. In this culture of simplicity and non-interference, people engaging in subterfuge become apparent, and their strategies are rendered ineffective.

Uniting the group into a team

The enlightened leader makes it their business to help everyone in the organisation towards fulfilment and higher attainment, not just those that seem somehow worthy of preferment. Lesser performers are also regarded as valuable members of the group who can be helped forward with education and other opportunities. This transforms a group into a team who are united behind the leader, and in whom the desire to collaborate is strong.

Avoid Machiavellian strategies

The enlightened leader refrains from clever strategies and political manoeuvrings. They know that this sends a message to do likewise, leading to an escalating cycle of such behaviour in the organisation. The enlightened leader therefore acts with simplicity and directness and so encourages the people to do likewise.

Humility

The enlightened leader understands that to rise above people in a leadership sense, they must remain below them by acting and speaking with sincere humility. This is perceived as complete identification with the people, engendering trust because the people instinctively know that if the leader is below them, the interests of the leader will be the same as theirs. If the leader does not act superior, the people see themselves in the leader and this engenders respect, if not love.

Compassion

The best kind of leader is compassionate, modest and does not thrust themselves into the lime-light. Lao Tzu considered that compassion in a person has a mysterious and deeply transformative effect on the mind of the person and those they come in contact with. Compassion endows the ability to have a lasting effect on the world. The enlightened leader therefore manifests compassion in their dealings with the world.

Using the Tao to influence group dynamics

The factors discussed here contribute to the harmonious achievement of goals at all levels, including the family, community, organisation, state, nation all the way up to the global the community of humanity.

Avoid self-aggrandisement

Enlightened people avoid being too visible or boastful of their achievements because there is a levelling mechanism in group psychology that naturally seeks to balance aggrandisement. Such behaviour creates excess. It creates instability in the social dynamic. Excess indicates that something has reached its peak and must by necessity go into decline. The enlightened person discretely removes themselves from the situation before the limelight shines upon them. For example, even the most popular political leader is harshly criticised by sections of the public, regardless of how diligently they work to stay in favour.

Hypocrisy is particularly poisonous. The enlightened person carefully avoids not only being a hypocrite, but the appearance of being one. They know it is tempting to agree with people in private discussions, expressing a different opinion with each person, as a way of earning their support. But the enlightened person knows that they must maintain the integrity of their position, and not vary it between people. This sameness of bearing towards everyone generates trust. Even though this may not please everyone, it does earn the enlightened person a reputation for integrity and impartiality. Often, the person of integrity pleases no-one, and is criticised for it because they refuse to take sides in a dispute. It is the only viable way to behave however, since any favours earned through double-dealing are short-lived. The friend of today becomes an enemy tomorrow. The person of integrity earns the respect of all, if not their friendship.

Avoid cunning and manipulation

Clever schemes and coercive force will often produce the opposite of what was planned, earning the person a reputation for cunning and duplicity. The enlightened person knows it is better to act with simple honesty in pursuit of one's goals, thus generating trust.

Simplicity is achieved through spontaneous, intuitive action based on an understanding of human nature and the situation at hand. This is the opposite of the Machiavellian ploy that may succeed in the short-term, but not in the mid to long-term.

Avoid aggression

Aggression in all of its forms is avoided by the enlightened person, since aggression creates excess, and excess always produces a neutralising reaction. Where affirmative action is called for, the enlightened person behaves assertively, not crossing the line between aggression and assertion. Assertion is restrained action.

Aggression in individuals and groups consumes much energy and resources, leading to resource depletion and weakening. Restrained action uses that energy constructively in the pursuit of its goals. The enlightened person knows that success does not have to come at the expense of another. The *win-win* scenario in which everyone benefits is in keeping with the Tao.

Use force only when absolutely necessary

When circumstances demand it, the use of force can be unavoidable. The enlightened person expresses regret at having to use force. They make it clear that it gives them no pleasure. As in Nature, the incidence of overwhelming force is rare (for example a tornado or earthquake). Most of the time, change is brought about through harmonious transformation.

Cultivating restraint and humility

Powerful organisations have much, but they also have much to lose. Their wealth and influence are the envy of others who want some of it for themselves. Such organisations can avoid this by cultivating modesty. They make themselves vulnerable to decline through complacency, excess, and sense of entitlement. Hubris leads them to believe they are unassailable. Any advantages the organisation possesses are kept concealed, out of sight from the external world where they will excite no envy or alarm.

Knowing how much is enough

Greed is a serious character flaw. It leads a person to not only desire more possessions, but to seek an identity for themselves in those possessions rather than focus on internal growth. When organisations are run without acquisitiveness as its central concern the internal qualities of the organisation are encouraged to grow in positive, self-improving ways. Its dealings with the world will take on a benevolent aspect which is likely to produce greater prosperity for all and limit the potential for harm.

Avoiding escalation

In any evolving social environment there will be conflict between opposing ideas. The enlightened person knows that the ideas that eventually prevail are those whose proponents have managed to avoid strong counter-reactions to the idea. They do this by avoiding aggression. Force is met with force, and strategy with strategy. Lao Tzu thought that the side that was wise enough to feel sorrow and regret at the use of force would be the side that triumphs.

Accepting blame

The enlightened person in organisations takes on the qualities of water. Soft and receptive with no edge and no form, water absorbs and transforms hard structures. By taking responsibility, including accepting the blame for situations, the enlightened person establishes their position at the centre of the organisation. They extend their influence outwards in a positive way. Blame in this context refers to that which happens inside and outside the organisation. They are able to foresee and avoid similar problems in the future.

Promoting independence

Lao Tzu considered the ideal social grouping (at every level from family to nation) to be one in which every member can reach their potential in whichever direction that takes them. They have access to health care, education and recreation. Nothing short of the pursuit of happiness. Every person values their life, so they will value life-enhancing activities that they instinctively know is the way to find themselves, develop a strong sense of purpose and ultimately reach their full potential. When a person feels strong and independent they are likely to work hard, maintain good relationships and remain loyal to the organisation.

Using the Tao to refrain from action

Strategic non-action can be a powerful method of achieving lasting influence in worldly affairs. In cultures where action is favoured over inaction, direct action is considered a virtue while inaction is considered little more than laziness or cowardice. This section suggests that there is a time for both action and inaction and describes the ways in which inaction can be used to advantage.

Selflessness

Periods of action are followed by a periods of inaction. To create a situation in which action is required, the enlightened person begins with inaction to prepare the way. The transition from inaction to action then seems natural, effortless. Such a beginning to action is unlikely to attract opposition. By placing themselves last and outside, the enlightened person creates a situation where natural social forces compel them forward towards the centre, doing so with naturalness and ease. Placing themselves selflessly will align their goals more closely with the evolving social environment.

Harmony

There is an inner pattern to everything in Nature. Cells-replicate, crystals grow, societies evolve all according to a precise template that resides, unseen, within the entity. Therefore the enlightened person is careful not to interfere with natural processes, knowing that to do so would be dangerous and ultimately futile. In social systems, the enlightened person maintains a position that is in harmony with the evolutionary forces that gradually evolve that society. Their influence is subtly exerted through the force of their focussed inner awareness. Thus they often refrain from taking action when to do so would adversely impact the natural evolutionary flow.

Avoid becoming too specialised

Lao Tzu considered that increasing specialisation is ultimately self-limiting because highly specialised systems impose constraints upon participants which effectively reduces them to machines forced to follow strict procedures. In such an environment, a person stops growing, stops being creative. In Nature, species that become too specialised are prone to extinction. So too with overly specialised organisations. Better to move towards universality, away from differentiation. By looking for what is universally true, one achieves simplicity. The greater the truth, the more simply it can be expressed.

Subtle influence

Lao Tzu observed that many of the troubles of the world are reactions to earlier provocations. People or groups seek revenge, and in doing so, set up a situation in which the trouble is perpetuated. What you resist persists. By refraining from action, the trouble dissipates over time. The enlightened person therefore uses subtle influence to resolve problems by choosing a course of non-action or minimal action designed to produce no further reactions.

Strategic non-action

A deep understanding of situations is gained from one's Intuition in a context of non-interference. The knowledge that derives from action is situation-specific, a deeper understanding is obscured by the interplay of action and reaction. Non-action or non-interference is therefore a strategic approach to harmonising one's inner awareness with the larger forces at work in the external world. This allows the enlightened person to instinctively know where best to position themselves to achieve their goals.

Truth in non-action

The enlightened person rids themselves of fixed ideas from the past, and centres their thinking in the Now, giving them a moment-by-moment awareness of how their social environment is evolving. This awareness reveals the possibilities that the evolving environment offers. Fixed ideas obscure such impressions. Ideally, one gains pure information from observing an environment that is not reacting to the observer in any way. If the observer is also an actor, then some of what is observed is due to the observer's own actions, leading to observational bias.

Being non-confrontational

Being infant-like is often used to describe the essence of the Tao. An infant and young child lives moment-by-moment in touch with their original nature before the layers of societal conditioning accumulate later in childhood. Because young children are clear embodiments of the Tao, the world is not inclined to harm them, nor do they struggle for wealth and power and so place themselves in harm's way. The enlightened person likewise adopts a spontaneous, natural, non-confrontational attitude towards life in order to protect themselves from harm in the world. When someone pushes them, they yield. Their opponent is thus thrown off balance and appears to the rest of the world as aggressive, which may then mobilise a neutralising reaction. The enlightened person concentrates on maintaining balanced energy. They know that unbalanced energy is inherently unstable and leads to its own demise

Like a river finding its way through a valley of boulders

When the enlightened person finds themselves in the position of needing to influence an on-going event they apply their efforts to the weakest area. When the weakness absorbs the effort, the weakness moves to another location, and the enlightened person follows. In this way they avoid confrontation with an apparently insurmountable problem and so avoid the counter-reactions that derive from the confrontation. They act like a river finding its way through a valley of stones. When the water encounters a stone, it flows smoothly around it and continues on. Eventually the water wears down the stone with little apparent effort. So it is that with non-confrontational actions, the enlightened person influences an on-going event. Their restrained action causes no adverse counter-reaction and they achieve their goals with apparent ease.

Recognising the beginning

The best time to influence events is at the beginning, before they acquire momentum. The enlightened person hones their skill at recognising when a situation is at its least entrenched state, and positions themselves to guide the event through to a successful conclusion. This skill is developed by limiting their desires and avoiding dogmatic or process-driven ways of accomplishing goals.

Give me freedom or give me death

Lao Tzu believed that human nature is essentially good. To remain good-hearted though, people need to perceive themselves as being free to live their lives how they see fit, to think the way they want to think, and not to have these freedoms eroded by authority figures and governments seeking to limit their freedoms and control them. When authority becomes oppressive, people lose the fear of death and rise up to end the oppression even if they lose their lives in the process. This is how precious freedom is in the hearts of people. For example, the French, Russian and American Revolutions all derived from people finding their rulers intolerable.

The doomed leader

An insecure leader believes their personal interests are identical to the interests of the organisation. They *are* the organisation. It causes them to curtail people's freedom. They are worried that given enough freedom, the people will oust them (a not unreasonable belief).

As the regime becomes more oppressive, the people suffer. Perhaps they have to work long hours in poor conditions. Maybe people do not get enough to eat, or disease goes untreated. All the while contempt for the leader grows. There can be only one outcome – the leader's eventual demise. The enlightened leader refrains from limiting people's freedom. Instead they provide the people with the means to grow and fulfil their potential, giving them the space in which to express that potential.

Chapter 3 The leadership literature

Until 'kings were philosophers or philosophers were kings' there will be injustice in the world. (Plato)

This chapter reviews the mostly modern literature, both practitioner and academic, on the broad subject of leadership. It is included in a book that deals in large part with the ancient thinking on leadership as a comparison. It can be seen that the underlying principles remain the same, with the outward form that the principles take being shaped by the cultural context in which they are expressed.

Around the same time as Lao Tzu was writing the Tao Te Ching, a world away in the Mediterranean the ancient Greeks were busy developing ideas and modalities that are the bedrock of western civilisation.

The philosopher Plato (427-347 BC) in his renowned dialogue *The Republic* outlined certain leadership principles that Western administrative thinking has based itself upon (Takala, 1998). Plato developed systematic administrative thinking for the efficient running of the city-sate (polis) which over time allowed the evolution of democracy. Plato described in detail the appropriate relationship between the State and individual citizens. This relationship was so close that it was not possible to think of a citizen living outside of his State.

The purpose (telos) of this State is to educate people to become 'good'. The State is like the human body in which

58

parts complement each other and act harmoniously. In terms of organisational theory, Plato would be regarded as a pre-modern functionalist.

In perhaps his best known tract *The Republic* (Polis), Plato states that politicians are the rulers of the new ideal state because they have (or should have) real knowledge (episteme) of what is 'the form of good'.

The art of ruling (leadership) can be based on scientific principles. In other words, it can be learned. The leader (ruler) uses the dialectic method to rationally analyse situations to determine appropriate courses of action with wisdom and understanding.

Distinguishing leaders and managers

The terms leader and manager are sometimes used interchangeably, adding to the ambiguity surrounding the study of leadership. Yet studies of administrative science usually find the terms differentiated. How is this done?

Chaos and order. Abraham Zeleznik (2004) in his seminal paper on leadership suggests that the differences between managers and leaders lie at a deep level of the human psyche. Attitudes towards chaos and order are the basis of the difference. A manager aims for stability and control, seeking to resolve problems quickly, sometimes at the cost of understanding the nature of the problem fully. Leaders, by contrast, accept or at least tolerate chaos and lack of structure so that they might perceive and come to understand the underlying causes of situations. In this sense, Zeleznik argues, leaders have more in common with creative thinkers such as artists and scientists than they do with managers.

According to Takala what managers and leaders have in common is the ability to get things done. Takala distinguishes them by seeing managers as a kind of instructor who puts pieces together, and then manages the 'things'. A manager is primarily concerned with making an organisation function by evolving routines that serve the ongoing and sometimes changing purposes of the organisation. Takala observes that management is an activity typical in *larger* corporations. But there is leadership in *every* organisation, and not only in business organisations. A leader is a person who takes care of people and emphasises in his/her activities the social psychology of the organisation. Takala notes that this is a somewhat artificial but commonplace distinction made in the management literature between the two activities. He acknowledges however that a person who runs a business or leads an organisation acts situationally in both roles, sometimes a manager, sometimes a leader.

Social construct of leadership

The socially constructed view holds that leadership is a myth, a socially constructed agency that reinforces existing social beliefs about the need for hierarchy (Gemmil and Oakley, 1996). A consequence of this view is the de-skilling of people, the placing of them into positions of subservience in order that they might follow the leader. Evidence of this is seen in the popular wish for heroes and messianic figures who will save the people and usher in a brighter future.

Despite the rather bleak nature of this position, it can nonetheless be observed that members of some organisations do behave like 'alienated robots' in their work relationships.

Leadership qualities of great groups

Bennis and Beiderman (1997) discuss at length the leadership qualities required in Great Groups. They observe that the nature of group leaders can vary widely. There are facilitators, doers, contrarians. Leaders are catalytic completers; taking on roles that nobody else plays and that are needed for the group to achieve its goal. They have an intuitive understanding of the 'chemistry' of the group and the dynamics of the work process. Furthermore they encourage dissent in the establishment and maintenance of a shared vision. They can distinguish between healthy, creative dissent and self-serving obstructionism.

Bennis and Beiderman (1997) identify four behavioral traits of effective group leaders:

- **Provide direction and meaning**. Group members are kept up-to-date on what is important and why their work makes a difference.

- **Generate and sustain trust**. The group has trust in itself and its leadership. This allows members to accept dissent and tolerate the turbulence of the group process.

- **Display a bias toward action, risk taking, and curiosity**. A sense of urgency and willingness to risk failure to achieve results.

- **Are purveyors of hope**. Find tangible and symbolic ways to demonstrate that the group can overcome difficulties.

Competencies of effective leaders

Bennis (1994) in a wide-ranging study determined that effective leaders display four distinct personality traits, and five specific competencies, the sum of which tends to manifest in strong and effective leadership:

Personality Traits	Competencies
Guiding vision	Technical competence
Passion	Interpersonal skills
Integrity	Conceptual skills
Daring	Judgment
	Character

No pairing order is implied by this table, it is a listing only.

Table 1: Traits of Effective Leaders.

Bennis (1999a) asserts that it is *character* that is the essential element determining a leader's effectiveness, saying *'leaders rarely fail because of technical incompetence'* but more so for lack of character (1999b).

Strong character can manifest in positive and negative ways, as the lessons of history inform us. Strong character makes for a strong leader, but character can be strong and negative/destructive. Offerman et al (2001) relates that a person's character will be determined by the sum total of his or her values. They identified the source of an employee's dissatisfaction and disillusionment is often the particular values held by leaders and the actions that these values motivate.

Davis and Landa (1999) surveyed workers across Canada, determining that 75% of Canadian employees did not trust their employers. Bennis (1999b) confirms the importance of trust by emphasising that employee confidence in leadership is critical in the workplace, saying that it is *'the emotional glue that can bond people to an organization.'*

Branham (2005) surveyed 3,149 people who voluntarily quit their job to assess their reasons for leaving. The exiting employees cited the following common reasons:

- Disappointment,
- Frustration,
- Anger,
- Disillusionment,
- Resentment, and
- Betrayal

These negative emotions are thought to be responses to an unmet human need for:

- Trust,

- Hope,

- A sense of worth, and

- The need to feel competent

It might therefore follow that an effective leader is someone who is able to meet these fundamental human needs, avoiding the trap that awaits a less effective leader.

Effective management of technical people

The figure of Watts Humphrey looms large in the history of software engineering. His contributions include the original Software Capability Maturity Model CMM-SW), Team Software Process (TSP) and Personal Software Process (PSP); all of which were developed while with the Software Engineering Institute's Process Program.

A lesser known, but nonetheless relevant work by Humphrey is *Managing Technical People* (1997). While this work is based on Humphrey's experience as a senior project manager with the IBM Corporation, rather than on empirical research, it serves as a validation device for empirical research, given his undoubted stature in the software engineering domain. 'Validation' is used here in the software engineering sense, meaning to check the truth and accuracy of something in the practical world.

To summarise the behaviors and qualities of effective managers of technical teams, Humphrey (1997) observes that:

- **Vision**. The ability to clearly perceive a worthy goal in terms of organisational success, and which has the quality of making people want to be part of the effort to make it real.

- **Goals**. Identified from the vision and the ability to drive steadfastly towards their realisation.

- **Conviction**. The ability to overcome obstacles in the path towards goal achievement.

- **Attract followers**. The ability to persuade others to sign-up or otherwise commit to a project, subject to limitations of choice. Humphrey distinguishes between the power to control and the power to lead. The latter is a mutual relationship, while the former implies coercion.

- **Care about followers**. A leader manifests an interest in the lives of, and a concern for the well-being of those they lead (what has been called 'individualised consideration').

- **Transform followers**. To convince followers to dedicate themselves to a project, sometimes requiring great personal effort, the net effect of which is to transform all concerned into high-achievers who derive much satisfaction from the transformative process (elsewhere described as transformational leadership).

- **Transact followers.** Use transactional power (power to reward with increased salary, promotion, job assignments) to effectively motivate followers.

- **Lead from below.** The ability to motivate followers to act as leaders in their own jobs, regardless of how modest or limited in scope this may be. The cumulative effect is nonetheless powerful.

Underlying qualities of effective leaders

The qualities that inspire people to persevere in the face of great difficulty, that engender trust and a sense of worth among team members are not always readily identifiable. These are qualities that are not easily detected, but which are found in the best of leaders.

Champy (2003) identify these underlying qualities as:

- Empathy,

- Personal responsibility, and

- Openness to discovering truth

Empathy

Macaluso (2003) suggests that empathy is the secret weapon of corporate success, an indispensable quality for any successful leader. Empathy is described as the ability to see the world through another's eyes, to experience it as they would. 'To walk a mile in another's shoes'. Macaluso says 'They use it to form strong relationships, pick up early warning signs, and recognize opportunities to influence.' It is this caring aspect of the leader that makes people want to stay with them, inspiring loyalty.

Personal responsibility

Effective leaders accept that the circumstances in which they find themselves are largely the result of their own previous actions. They recognise the cause and effect relationships that have created the current situation, and understand how to engineer future desirable effects by performing certain actions in the present. They do not blame others (Macaluso, 2003). They are able to see how their behavior affects corporate vision and how their leadership can affect the profitability of the organisation. Effective leaders are proactive, rather than reactive, taking the initiative to improve matters.

Open to the truth

Effective leaders fearlessly search for truth, knowing that sometimes the truth will not be pleasant to face (Macaluso, 2003). They encourage discussion and do not resile from the outcomes of those discussions. The value of truth is recognised as the supreme antidote to delusion, or wishful thinking.

Macaluso concludes with the point that really effective leaders are those that maximise human capital by displaying empathy, personal responsibility and truthfulness in all of their dealings. These traits appear to engender in people a favourable emotional state that is the foundation for effective team operation.

Transformational vs. Transactional

Zhang et al (2005) identify two parallel dimensions of leadership: *transformational vs. transactional*, and *participative vs. directive*. These have been derived from a body of foundational work in the area of leadership styles in a virtual team context.

On the Transformational / Transactional dimension we see the Transformational element as comprising four behavioral components (Bass, 1985; Bass et al, 1987; Lowe et al 1996):

- **Charisma or idealized influence**. The leader engenders in the members a sense of pride, respect, faith and respect, together with a sense of purpose/mission.

- **Individualized consideration**. The leader manifests a deep concern for the well-being of team members, and provides mentoring.

- **Intellectual stimulation**. The leader stimulates members to think in original ways, emphasising the triumph of reason over irrationality, and challenging established ways of thinking.

- **Inspirational motivation**. The leader creates high standards, communicating high expectations.

- Continuing with the Transformational / Transactional dimension we see the Transactional element as comprising three behavioral elements[28] [29] [30]:

- **Contingent reward**. The leader rewards performance on the basis of it having fulfilled prescribed obligations.

- **Management-by exception**. The leader ensures the standards are met.

- **Management-by-exception (passive).** The leader adopts a *laissez-faire* attitude until non-compliance of standards has occurred.

Participative vs. directive

On the participative vs. directive dimension, Bass (1990) defines participative leadership as the equalization of power and sharing of problem solving with followers by consulting them before making a decision.

Bass (1990) defines directive leadership as providing and seeking compliance with directions for accomplishing a problem solving task. Participative leadership and directive leadership are considered parallel to transformational leadership and transactional leadership respectively.

Review of leadership findings

Zhang et al (2005) discuss at length the findings from various literatures about the distinctions that can be made between Transformational / Transactional and Participative / Directive Leadership styles. In particular, they relate the following:

Bass and Avolio (1993) discuss that in general, supportive, encouraging communication from the leader to team members were made under participative leadership rather than directive leadership. In dealing with a semi-structured or poorly defined problem, proposed solutions were more forthcoming in a participative leadership situation. On the other hand, solutions to structured or well-defined problems were more forthcoming with directive leadership.

In terms of group effectiveness or potency, higher level transformational leadership resulted in greater effectiveness than lower levels of transformational leadership (Kahai et al, 1997). The group potency difference was larger when groups were engaged in interdependent tasks rather than independent tasks. Interdependence resulted in greater potency. Anonymous groups working under high transformational leadership and identified groups working under low transformational leadership were most effective.

Elaboration (or the extent to which work was developed to a higher degree of complexity) was observed to improve significantly; while originality improved marginally when higher levels of transformational leadership were present (George et al, 1994). Moreover, identified groups or teams with high transformational leadership were more flexible than identified groups in low transformational situations. Flexibility tended to vanish when groups were anonymous.

Lim et al (1994) indicate that anonymity by itself does not alter the effects of leadership style on (a) participation, (b) cooperation or (c) the originality of the solution. With transactional leadership, anonymity was negatively associated with participation and association due to social loafing (idle chit-chat, gossip etc), but it was positively related to originality of solutions when a group reward as opposed to an individual reward situation exists. It appears that giving members time to engage in apparently idle communication when group-based solutions are rewarded results in more focussed outcomes. With transformational leadership, anonymity did not significantly change the rate or degree of participation, cooperation, and originality when a group rewards situation exists (as opposed to an individual rewards condition). Team member satisfaction with the leader did not apparently differ across leadership styles; however transactional leadership did appear to result in greater group efficacy and task satisfaction than does transformational leadership. These advantages associated with transactional leadership (over transformational leadership) diminished when anonymity was introduced.

Team members working under the influence of transformational leaders tended to produce quality over quantity (Avolio et al, 2000). Output improved, though the quantity of it decreased. Members also tended to be more satisfied and displayed greater group cohesiveness than those led by transactional leaders. Leadership satisfaction (highest in the face-to-face setting) was relatively high in virtual environments that approached full-immersion.

Transformational leadership was associated with higher levels of trust in the leader and value congruence.

McColl-Kennedy and Anderson (2002) report that both participative and directive leaderships were positively related to degree of participation. These in turn produced higher team performance, but with paradoxically lower levels of leadership satisfaction. The positive relationship between participation and team performance as well as the negative relationship between participation and team performance became stronger as the problem turned to be less structured.

Leadership of virtual teams

The concept and practice of distributed work is not new, enjoying a long and colourful history as discussed by O'Leary et al (2002) in their extended case study of the Hudson Bay Company from 1670 to 1826. Yet it has been the advent and subsequent advances in communications technology that has been a critical enabler of the development of this organisational form and practice (Ahuja et al, 1997).

It has been observed (Cascio and Shurygailo, 2003) that distributed teams, (or virtual teams as they might be called), face particular problems in relation to leadership. Organisational and management research has focussed intensively on the issue of leadership, as seen in a previous section, yet there is relatively little research done thus far on the emerging challenge of leadership in virtual teams.

Leadership of knowledge workers

Discussion of leadership in the globalized economy of the 21st century is not complete without examination of the way in which the new generation of workers who contribute to the global economy are best led and managed. Arguably, project team members on complex virtual teams fall into the category of knowledge worker for the reasons discussed below.

Knowledge workers are broadly defined as persons contributing to the knowledge economy (a post-industrial, post-service economic system). They are self-motivated, challenge-seeking persons who capture, manipulate and apply knowledge to create value. Knowledge workers usually know more about their job than their manager or anyone else in the organisation, and who often do not consider themselves to be subordinates in the traditional sense (DuBrin et al, 2006). Knowledge workers cannot therefore be managed/lead in the same way as industrial or service workers.

One of Australia's leading academics, Professor Glyn Davis is recognised as an outstanding leader in a knowledge environment, having been described in those terms by former Queensland Premier Peter Beattie (DuBrin, 2006). Professor Davis, who is currently the Vice Chancellor of Melbourne University, says that leaders should not tell knowledge workers what to do, but rather need to understand *what* they do and then lead by persuasive vision. This can be effected by:

- The views and visions of the knowledge workers are aggregated and shaped into a consistent theme,

- A vision based on these embedded values is developed,

- The vision thus formulated is articulated *back* to the knowledge workers with empathy and enthusiasm,

- The leader demonstrates high credibility,

- An understanding of the business and,

- Clear support for the business,

- The leader must be perceived as the embodiment of the values of the organisation,

- The leader skilfully uses multiple channels of communication to convey a consistent message that makes people feel good about working for the organisation. (This sounds similar to Eisenhower's idea of leadership being about *getting people to want to do what it is you want them to do*).

Skryme (1998) outline some guidelines for the leadership of knowledge workers, distilled from the management literature. At a high-level, the critical leadership factors are a well articulated vision, a clear understanding of the link between knowledge and business benefits, together with effective marketing promotion. The leader must have a deep belief in the value of knowledge management to the organisation, and a commitment to innovative thinking and acting (including the willingness to commit resources).

DuBrin et al (2006) summarise the leadership factors for knowledge workers as follows:

- Individual development plans for staff,

- Acquisition of innovative projects,

- Team composition; multi-disciplinary roles and mentoring/coaching,

- Use of quality systems,

- Systematic project evaluations,

- Planning for both formal and informal communications,

- Culture in which success and failure are discussed openly,

- Specific knowledge may become redundant but the ability to learn always remains valuable to the organisation,

- Knowledge workers' values must be aligned with those of the organisation,

Effective virtual team leadership

Zhang, Fjermestad and Tremaine (2005) in their review of earlier virtual team leadership studies suggest that given the inconsistencies inherent in the results, that a 'contingency' approach to studying team leadership might be appropriate. Contingency in this context refers to there being no single set of leadership skills that bring about effective virtual team leadership; rather that effectiveness is contingent upon contextual variables and situational complexity.

The contextual variables identified by Zhang, Fjermestad and Tremaine (2005) from their review of the literature include:

Communication media richness facilitating Trust. The technology's ability to provide an environment that provides a rich perceptual experience for the participants. This includes immediate feedback, the number of perceptual cues and communication channels used, and the personalization of messages. Media richness facilitates trust between leadership and team member by minimising team process degradation while maximising motivation and commitment to a successful project outcome.

Goal-frustrating events managed by Optimism. Obstacles and set-backs like technical problems, deadline pressures that threaten the accomplishment of the prescribed project objectives. This creates negative affect among team members, which can amplify itself over time to create a significant problem for the team. Inspirational motivation, optimism, individualized consideration and contingent reward all appear to optimise team performance by creating a positive affective climate.

Leader/follower gender, improved individualised consideration. Female leaders have been shown to improve virtual team performance by exhibiting a higher degree of Individualized consideration behavior which causes higher levels of team satisfaction with the leadership. Combining individualized consideration with contingent reward further improves the leadership effectiveness of female virtual team leaders. In addition, in female-only groups, the effect of a charismatic virtual team leader is enhanced through effective trust-building.

Sloan Distributed Leadership Model

Ancona, Malone, Orlikowski and Senge (2006) at the Sloan School of Management have developed a Distributed Leadership Model that offers an approach to understanding and practicing leadership.

The Sloan Model basically outlines four dimensions of leadership:

Sense making: the process of making sense of the world around us, understanding the context in which we are operating:

- Get data from multiple sources: customers, suppliers, employees, competitors, other departments, and investors.

- Involve others in your sense making. Say what you think you are seeing, and check with people who have different perspectives from yours.

- Use early observations to shape small experiments in order to test your conclusions. Look for new ways to articulate alternatives and better ways to understand options.

- Do not simply apply existing frameworks but instead be open to new possibilities. Try not to describe the world in stereotypical ways, such as good guys and bad guys, victims and oppressors, or marketers and engineers.

Relating: developing strategic relationships within and across organizations:

- Spend time trying to understand others' perspectives, listening with an open mind and without judgment.

- Encourage others to voice their opinions. What do they care about? How do they interpret what's going on? Why?

- Before expressing your ideas, try to anticipate how others will react to them and how you might best explain them.

- When expressing your ideas, don't just give a bottom line; explain your reasoning process.

- Assess the strengths of your current connections: How well do you relate to others when receiving advice? When giving advice? When thinking through difficult problems? When asking for help?

Visioning: creating a compelling and feasible vision of the future as it might apply to the organization:

- Practice creating a vision in many arenas, including your work life, your home life, and in community groups. Ask yourself, 'What do I want to create?'

- Develop a vision about something that inspires you. Your enthusiasm will motivate you and others. Listen to what they find exciting and important.

- Expect that not all people will share your passion. Be prepared to explain why people should care about your vision and what can be achieved through it. If people don't get it, don't just turn up the volume. Try to construct a shared vision.

- Don't worry if you don't know how to accomplish the vision. If it is compelling and credible, other people will discover all sorts of ways to make it real –ways you never could have imagined on your own.

- Use images, metaphors, and stories to convey complex situations that will enable others to act.

Inventing: creating new ways of working together to realize the vision:

- Don't assume that the way things have always been done is the best way to do them.

- When a new task or change effort emerges, encourage creative ways of getting it done.

- Experiment with different ways of organizing work. Find alternative methods for grouping and linking people.

- When working to understand your current environment, ask yourself, 'What other options are possible?'

All of the previous paragraphs derived from Ancona, Malone, Orlikowski and Senge, (2007).

The authors go on to describe the indications of when these activities are not being performed well:

Signs of weak sense making:

- You feel strongly that you are usually right and others are often wrong.

- You feel your views describe reality correctly, but others' views do not.

- You find you are often blindsided by changes in your organization or industry.

- When things change, you typically feel resentful. (that's not the way it should be!)

Signs of weak relating:

- You blame others for failed projects.

- You feel others are constantly letting you down or failing to live up to your expectations.

- You find that many of your interactions at work are unpleasant, frustrating, or argumentative.

- You find many of the people you work with untrustworthy.

Signs of weak visioning:

- You feel your work involves managing an endless series of crises.

- You feel like you're bouncing from pillar to post with no sense of larger purpose.

- You often wonder, 'Why are we doing this?' or 'Does it really matter?'

- You can't remember the last time you talked to your family or a friend with excitement about your work.

Signs of weak inventing:

- Your organization's vision seems abstract to you.

- You have difficulty relating your company's vision to what you are doing today.

- You notice dysfunctional gaps between your organization's aspirations and the way work is organized.

- You find that things tend to revert to business as usual.

All of the previous paragraphs derived from Ancona, Malone, Orlikowski and Senge, (2007).

Chapter 4 Self-Actualisation & Leadership

The humanistic psychologist Abraham Maslow is well-known for his ideas on a hierarchy of human needs. These are represented in a pyramid shape, with self-actualisation at the pyramid's apex.

The achievement of self-actualisation is recognised by Maslow as a human need. This need asserts itself once we have satisfied the lower-order needs for food, shelter, sex, then middle-order needs for safety and security, then love and belonging, and then the higher-order need for self-esteem. Self-actualisation comes next.

The annals of various religions tell us that a person can achieve enlightenment with only some or none of the higher and middle order needs being met, and with only the barest of lower-order needs like food and shelter being satisfied. This is more difficult, requiring you to become an ascetic recluse and engage in mortification of the flesh in order to free yourself of these normal human needs. This book is not recommending this course of action. Our body is not an impediment to self-actualisation.

Self-Actualised (SA) people, whoever they are and whatever the circumstances of their lives, tend to approach life in recognisable ways that can be described and perhaps emulated. Since there is a strong correspondence between the characteristics of effective leaders and SA people, and exploration of the characteristics of SA people serves as a fresh starting point in our investigation into the underlying nature of Leadership.

Experience life wholeheartedly, now

SA people throw themselves wholeheartedly into the experiences that come their way. You concentrate on the experience to the exclusion of all else. By investing fully in the moment, you receive back from the world in equal measure, thus heightening the experience further.

There is strong correspondence here with the Buddhist practice of Mindfulness in which your are fully present in the now moment. Your heightened awareness allows you to fully experience each moment on the understanding that *every moment is the best moment.*

Mindfulness is cultivated by *observing* one's own mind. It leads you to dwell in the present where life can actually be experienced, and not in the past or future where experiences can only be remembered or imagined.

In the Now you observe the world of phenomena in a judgment-free way. You accept it without mental resistance, understanding that this resistance is what prevents you from experiencing every moment as the best moment.

Being fully aware, SA people understand that Life is a series of moment-by-moment choices between *safety* (out of fear and need for defence) and *risk* (for the sake of progress and growth). You consciously make the growth choice many times a day.

Your primary reality is a rich inner life

SA people go beyond socially-defined modes of thinking, feeling and acting, letting their inner experience tell them what they truly feel.

SA people live rich inner lives which they recognise as their primary reality. The outer world is seen as their secondary reality. Hence they tend to socialise with those who do not demand sacrifice to group-norms as the price of friendship.

The need for social acceptance and a sense of belonging can lead people to think and act in conventional, group-defined ways. To gain the security of belonging to a group, the price is independence of thought and the sacrifice of true autonomy.

Honesty with oneself

It takes courage, but SA people look honestly at themselves and take responsibility for who they are and what happens in their life. They avoid feeling like a victim and remain empowered.

Self-delusion is the enemy of self-actualisation. Looking around in the world, it is rare to find people who do not delude themselves as a coping mechanism. SA people recognise that such coping mechanisms are ultimately self-defeating.

SA people achieve true empowerment through being honest with themselves, and having the courage to endure the pain that the honesty sometimes brings.

SA people have a superior ability to reason, to see the truth. They are realistically oriented with an efficient perception of reality extending into all areas of life. They are not frightened by the unknown.

SA people see the truth of the world, recognising the flawed and temporary nature of objects and ideas. They see the cause and effect relationships that connect the events of the world.

Listen to your own tastes

SA people are prepared to be unpopular if necessary. As mentioned previously, the need for social acceptance can lead one to compromise one's principles for the sake of getting along.

SA people understand that while compromise on minor issues is often necessary, there is a line that must not be crossed.

Know thyself

SA people ask themselves who are you, what are you, what is good and what is bad for you, where you are going, what is your mission? Opening up to oneself in this way means recognising one's defences--and then finding the courage to give them up.

SA people consciously live their lives in the ways listed above and so they allow their leadership potential to emerge and become established.

Accept the world as it is

SA people see human nature as is. They have rid themselves of crippling guilt or shame; they enjoy themselves without regret or apology, and have no unnecessary inhibitions.

SA people do not have high expectations, so they are rarely disappointed.

Original & unorthodox

SA people are unhampered by convention. Their ethics are autonomous, they see themselves as an individual, and are motivated towards continual improvement.

SA people respond to situations appropriately because they perceive the situation clearly and act accordingly, not by replaying a standard response from their behavioral repertoire.

A sense of purpose

SA people have a mission in life requiring much energy, and their mission is their reason to be alive. SA people are usually serene and worry-free as they pursue their mission with unshakeable determination.

Their sense of purpose informs almost every aspect of the SA person's life. It is their reason to get out of bed in the morning, and the cause of their gratitude for being alive in the world, even under less than ideal circumstances.

Private

SA people can be alone but not lonely. They are unflappable, retaining dignity amid confusion and personal misfortunes. The SA person is deeply introspective, and for this they require privacy, a calm place away from the chattering crowd.

The SA person's need for privacy is the source of their creative output without which they would be frustrated.

Autonomous

SA people are self-contained, resilient and stable in the face of hard knocks. They are independent from the love and respect of others in the sense that they can resist attempts to use these to manipulate them.

Autonomy does not mean being a law unto oneself. Rather it means being the embodiment of natural law, and as such do not need to look outside of themselves at some external authority to know how to act.

Peak experiences

In Maslow's words 'Feelings of limitless horizons opening up to the vision, the feeling of being simultaneously more powerful and also more helpless than one ever was before, the feeling of ecstasy and wonder and awe, the loss of placement in time and space with, finally, the conviction that something extremely important and valuable had happened, so that the subject was to some extent transformed and strengthened even in his daily life by such experiences. When peak experiences are especially powerful, the sense of self dissolves into an awareness of a greater unity.' (from *Religion, Values and Peak Experiences*, 1970).

Conclusion

A leader is arguably someone who has achieved a degree of self-actualisation. Those around the SA person perceive the qualities of personality that self-actualisation confers, and these are perceived in leadership terms.

Becoming a leader is therefore a journey of self-discovery and improvement, not an isolated act separate from other aspects of life.

Chapter 5 Evolutionary Psychology

Continuing the theme that leadership is an aspect of the Self-Actualised person, it might be reasonably assumed that learning how to transcend certain aspects of our base nature would be helpful in moving towards Self-Actualisation.

Evolutionary Psychology shows us what it is to be human, and more importantly how it is we come to be this way. The Environment of Evolutionary Adaptedness (EEA) in which humans evolved has programmed our basic responses to the world. For humans, our EEA is generally agreed to be the Pleistocene epoch of the Quaternary period, spanning around 1.8 million to 11 thousand years ago.

While the basic nature we evolved in the Pleistocene may have been helpful *during* that period, the modern world is significantly different to our EEA and some of those instinctive responses are no longer helpful or healthy.

Learning to distinguish the healthy instincts (like nurturing our children) from the unhealthy (like eating too much) helps us to adapt and optimise our life-style and move towards becoming a Self-Actualised person.

From an evolutionary perspective, the human ego can be understood as that aspect of a person's psyches that develops survival strategies. The ego is superb at this, it has enabled our species to survive and prosper in an often hostile Pleistocene.

89

The ego works by categorizing what it encounters in the world as being either helpful or harmful to its survival. That is the dualistic distinction that the ego instinctively makes. In doing so it creates a world of dualities, of polar opposites. The ego was necessary for survival.

The ego is strengthened and defined by conflict. While conflict can be real, the ego also creates conflict where none need exist as a way of strengthening itself. The world is full of people whose lives consist of one conflict-driven drama after another. They are locked in egoic thinking, dancing to the ancient war-drums that have been beating in the back of their minds since the Pleistocene.

But as humanity evolves to a higher level of consciousness, aided by civil society and technological advances, we begin to see that having solved or eliminated most of the problems and dangers that threatened our ancestors, egoic thinking as a survival mechanism is no longer as helpful as it once was. Take for example our instinct to eat salty/ fatty/ sweet foods so that we might store energy in body fat and have it in reserve the next time food is scarce.

Anthropologists say that in our evolutionary past it was impossible to find so much salty/ fatty/ sweet food that it would harm you, so we are programmed to eat as much of it as we can find, as often as possible. In today's world, we have to curb this tendency if we are not to become obese. Our higher rational self needs to recognize that seeing the world through the eyes of our primitive ancestors, with danger behind every bush, is no longer helpful to our well-being.

Consider the *Seven Deadly Sins*. Not to bring religion into the discussion, but the Seven Deadly Sins are a conveniently packaged example of the case in point. The catalogue of behaviors to avoid in this package include being angry, greedy, lazy, proud, lustful, envious and gluttonous. Behaving in any of these ways in the modern world is considered to be anti-social, not to mention hazardous to one's journey in the after-life.

Yet as harmful as the Seven Deadly Sins are in today's world, all of these behaviors would have improved our primitive ancestors' chances of survival:

Anger warns against attack, or acts as a stimulus to fight ferociously if actually attacked.

Greed leads a person acquire an abundance of useful commodities like food, weapons, shelter, reproductive partners, animal skins, access to drinking water etc, all of which improves their survival chances.

Sloth or laziness conserves energy. Food was scarce in the Pleistocene with its repeated Ice Ages; people would have been cold and hungry if not starving much of the time. Survival would have depended on conserving one's energy for the high-dividend activities like hunting or defence.

Pride enhances self-esteem which improves survivability because it leads an individual to value themselves more highly and so assert their right to claim and fight for the resources they need to survive.

Lust enhances the desire to reproduce and pass one's genetic material on to the next generation.

Envy leads a person to acquire other people's goods on the assumption that if the others value the goods enough to obtain them in the first place, they are worth trying to get for oneself.

Gluttony takes advantage of abundant food, while it lasts, to lay down fat reserves to help an individual through the famine that was always just around the corner for the Pleistocene human.

Quite simply, if you recognise how much of our behaviour derives from our primitive past, you are one step away from consciously choosing to not behave that way.

Some of our instincts still serve us well; for example the instinct to love and nurture our children, to avoid various dangers and to seek life-affirming opportunities. By being fully aware, we can choose to continue behavior that is helpful, and discontinue that which is unhelpful on our path towards Self-Actualisation.

We must therefore learn to put our ego in its proper place as a survival tool from our evolutionary past that need not be used unless our survival is threatened. In place of the ego is an on-going awareness that the world and everyone in it is connected to and dependant upon the whole, rather than seeing the world as a disconnected and dangerous place. The ego is a practical aspect of who we are, useful at times, but not the totality of who were are, and certainly not what should be in the driver's seat.

This book has presented a perspective on Leadership that places it as a characteristic of a fully aware, self-actualised person, someone who is in the process of achieving their very considerable potential as a human being. Leadership is how the world recognises people who are moving towards becoming their Highest Self.

Chapter 6 References

The following is a representative list of publications in the practitioner and academic press for the further reading of interested parties:

Ahuja, M. K., Carley, K., & Galletta, D. F. (1997). *Individual performance in distributed design groups: An empirical study.* Paper presented at the SIGCPR Conference, San Francisco. p 165.

Ancona, D., Malone, T., Orlikowski, W., Senge, P. (2007). *In Praise of the Incomplete Leader,* Harvard Business Review; Feb2007, Vol. 85 Issue 2, pp. 92-100.

Avolio, B., Kahai, S., George, E., (2000). *E-leadership: Implications for Theory, Research, and Practice,* Leadership Quarterly, vol. 11, pp.615-668.

Bass, B., (1985). *Leadership and Performance beyond Expectations,* New York: The Free Press.

Bass, B., Avolio, B. Goodheim, L., (1987). *Biography and the Assessment of Transformational Leadership at the World Class Level,* Journal of Management, vol. 13, pp. 7-19.

Lowe, K., Kroeck K., Sivasubramaniam, N, (1996). Effectiveness Correlates of Transformational and Transactional Leadership: a Meta-analytic Review of the MLQ Literature, Leadership Quarterly, vol. 7, pp. 385-425.

Bass, B, (1990). *Bass and Stodgill's Handbook of Leadership,* New York: Free Press.

References

Bass, B., Avolio, B., (1993). *Transformational Leadership: A response to Critiques*, in M. M. Chemers & R. Ayman (Eds.), Leadership theory and research: Perspectives and directions, pp. 49-80, San Diego, CA: Academic Press.

Bell, B.S., Kozlowski, S.W. (2002). *A Typology of Virtual Teams: Implications for Effective Leadership.* Group and Organisational Management, Vol. 27, No.1 pp. 14-19.

Bennis W., Beiderman P. (1997). Organizing Genius: The Secrets of Creative Collaboration. Addison-Wesley.

Bennis, W. (1999a). *The Leadership Advantage, Leader to Leader*, 12, p 12

Bennis, W. (1999b), *Five Competencies of New Leaders, Executive Excellence*, 16 (7), pp.4-5.

Bennis, W. and Nanus, B., (1985). *Leaders: the strategies for taking charge.* New York, Haper and Row.

Bennis, W. (1994). On Becoming a Leader, *What Leaders Read 1*, Perseus Publishing, p 2.

Box, G.E.P., (1979). *Robustness in the strategy of scientific model building, in Robustness in Statistics,* R.L. Launer and G.N. Wilkinson, Editors. Academic Press: New York.

Branham, L. (2005). The *7 Hidden Reasons Employees Leave*, American Management Association, 1st Edition, pp 19-20.

Cascio, W., Shurygailo, S., (2003). *E-Leadership and Virtual Teams, Organizational Dynamics,* vol. 31, pp. 362-376.

Champy, J. (2003), *The Hidden Qualities of Great Leaders, Fast Company Magazine,* 76, p 2.

References

Davis, T., Landa, M.J. (1999). *The Trust Deficit, Canadian Manager*, 21(1), pp. 10-27.

Deming, W.E., (2000). *Out of the Crisis*, MIT Press, Cambridge MA.

Drucker, P. (1996). *Managing in a Time of Great Change*, Butterworth Heinemann, London.

DuBrin, A., Dalglish, C., Miller, P (2006). *Leadership*, John Wiley, Australia, 2nd Edition, Brisbane.

Eisenhower, D. D. (1988). *The Eisenhower Diaries.* Edited by Robert H. Ferrell. New York: Norton.

Gemmill, G., Oakley, J., (1992). Leadership: An alienating social myth?, Human Relations, Vol. 45, Issue 2 pp. 113-129.

George, J., Easton, G. Jr., Nunamaker, J., and Northcraft, G., (1990). *A Study of Collaborative Work with and without Computer-based Support*, Information Systems Research, vol. 1, pp. 394-415.

Ho, T., Raman, K., (1997). *The Effect of GSS and Elected Leadership on Small Group Meetings*, Journal of Management Information Systems, vol. 23, pp. 409-472.

Holmstrom, H., Fitzgerald, B., Agerfalk, P., Conchuir, E., (2006). *Agile Practices Reduce Distance in Global Software Development.* Information Systems Management; Summer 200623;3, p 9.

Humphrey, W.S., (2002). *Winning with Software.* Addison Wesley Longman, Reading Massachusetts.

Humphrey, W.S., (2000). *Introduction to the Team Software Process.* Addison Wesley Reading Massachusetts, p19.

References

Humphrey, W.S., (1997). *Managing Technical People: innovation, teamwork, and the software process.* Addison Wesley Longman, Reading Massachusetts.

Kahai, S., Sosik, J. and Avolio, B. (1997). Effects of Leadership Style and Problem Structure on Work Group Process and Outcomes in an Electronic Meeting System Environment, Personnel Psychology, vol. 50, pp. 1-146.

Lim, L., Raman, K., Wei, K., (1994). *Interacting Effects of GSS and Leadership,* Decision Support System, vol. 12, pp. 199-1.

Macaluso, J. (2003). *Harnessing the Power of Emotional Intelligent Leadership,* The CEO Refresher, p 2.

McColl-Kennedy, J., Anderson, R., (2002). Subordinate manager Gender Combination and Perceived Leadership Style Influence on Emotions, Self-esteem and Organizational Commitment, Journal of Business Research, vol. 13, pp 545-559.

Offerman, L.R., Hanges, P.J. & Day, D.V. (2001). *Leaders, followers, and values; progress and prospects for theory and research, The Leadership Quarterly,* 12, pp. 129-131.

O'Leary, M., Orlikowski, W. J., & Yates, J. (2002). *Distributed work over the centuries: Trust and control in the Hudson's Bay Company, 1670–1826.* In P. Hinds & S. Kiesler (Eds.), Distributed Work: 27–54. Cambridge, MA: MIT Press.

Skryme, D., (1998). *Measuring the Value of Knowledge,* Business Intelligence Limited, Wimbledon, United Kingdom.

Takala, T., (1998). *Plato on Leadership.* Journal of Business Ethics 17: pp. 785-798

References

Yukl, G., (1994). *Leadership in Organisations*. Englewood Cliffs, N.J. Prentice-Hall.

Zaleznik, A., (2004*). Managers and Leaders: Are they different?*, Harvard Business Review, The Best of HBR edition, January. Article first published in 1977.

Zhang, S., Fjermestad, J., Tremaine, M., (2005). *Leadership Styles in Virtual Team Context: Limitations, Solutions and Propositions*, Proceedings of the 38th Hawaii International Conference on System Sciences.